Ch

—— B i b l e S t u d i e s ——

LOVING THE WORLD

Carolyn Nystrom

in 6 or 12 studies
for individuals or groups

With Notes for Leaders

INTERVARSITY PRESS
DOWNERS GROVE, ILLINOIS 60515

InterVarsity Press is the book-publishing division of InterVarsity Christian Fellowship, a student movement active on campus at hundreds of universities, colleges and schools of nursing in the United States of America, and a member movement of the International Fellowship of Evangelical Students. For information about local and regional activities, write Public Relations Dept., InterVarsity Christian Fellowship, 6400 Schroeder Rd., P.O. Box 7895, Madison, WI 53707-7895.

All Scripture quotations, unless otherwise indicated, are taken from the HOLY BIBLE, NEW INTERNATIONAL VERSION. Copyright © 1973, 1978, 1984 International Bible Society. Used by permission of Zondervan Publishing House. All rights reserved.

In study 2 questions 15, 17, 18, 20 and 22 were first published in Who Is Jesus? A Woman's Workshop on Mark, *Carolyn Nystrom (Grand Rapids: Zondervan, 1987), pp. 37-39.*

Cover photograph: Robert McKendrick

ISBN 0-8308-1143-5

Printed in the United States of America ∞

15	14	13	12	11	10	9	8	7	6	5	4	3	2
03	02	01	00	99	98	97	96	95	94				

Contents

Welcome to Christian Character Bible Studies

What is a Christian character? And how does one go about developing it?

As with most questions of faith and the practice of faith, the best source of information is the Bible itself. The Christian Character Bible Studies explore a wide variety of biblical passages that speak of character development.

The Bible speaks of love—love for ourselves, love for God, love for other believers, and love for those who do not yet believe.

The Bible speaks of responsibility—responsibility for the poor, responsibility for the weak, responsibility for the environment, responsibility for our assets, responsibility to work and responsibility to share our faith.

The Bible speaks of holy living—honesty, sexual purity, mental discipline, faithfulness, courage and obedience.

The Bible speaks of hope—a hope that is based on the character of God, the work of Jesus Christ, and an accurate view of our human limitations. It is a hope that says, "Residence on earth is temporary; residence in heaven is eternal."

This series of Bible study guides will help you explore, in

thought and in practice, these many facets of Christian character. But why bother? Why can't we accept ourselves the way we are? Isn't that the route to mental health? Not entirely. We are all in transition. Each new day brings new influences on who we are. We respond—and change. With God's help, that change can be toward Christian growth.

Growing in character is satisfying. It carries with it the sense of growing in godliness—into the image that God created us to be. It carries a sense of harmony, of walking hand in hand with God. But it is not painless. Therefore these guides will constantly ask us to hold up our character to the mirror of Scripture and to bend that character along the lines of Christ's image. God doesn't want us to stay the same. We should allow the Spirit to nudge us through these studies toward the spiritual maturity that God designed for his people.

What Kind of Guide Is This?

This is an inductive Bible study guide. That means that each study deals with a particular passage of Scripture and attempts to understand its content, its meaning, and its implications for godly living. A variety of questions will explore all three of those areas.

This is a thought-provoking guide. Each question assumes a variety of answers. Many questions do not have "right" answers, particularly questions that aim at meaning or application. Instead, the questions should inspire users to explore the passage in more depth.

This study guide is flexible—you can use it for individual study or in a group. You can vary the amount of time you take for each study, and you have various options for the number of studies you do from the guide. This is possible because every guide in this series is structured with two unique features. First, each of the six studies is divided into two parts, and second, several questions are marked with an asterisk (*), indicating that they may be

Guidelines for Using the Christian Character Bible Studies

Option	Type of Use	Time Allowed	Number of Sessions	Your Plan to Follow
1	Individual	30 minutes	12	Divide each study into two sessions, and use all the questions.
2	Individual	45 minutes	6	Use one study per session, and skip questions with an asterisk (*) if time doesn't allow for them.
3	Individual	60 minutes	6	Use one study per session, and use all the questions.
4	Group	30 minutes	12	Divide each study into two sessions, and skip questions with an asterisk(*) if time doesn't allow for them.
5	Group	45-60 minutes	12	Divide each study into two sessions, and use all the questions.
6	Group	60 minutes	6	Use one study per session, and skip questions with an asterisk (*) if time doesn't allow for them.
7	Group	90 minutes	6	Use one study per session, and use all the questions.

skipped if time does not allow for them. So you can have six sessions or twelve, with varying amounts of time to fit your needs.

How do you decide which approach is best for you? Looking at the chart on page 6, decide if you will be using this guide for individual study or in a group. Then determine how much time you want to spend on each session and how many sessions you want to have. Then follow the plan described in the far right column.

For example, if you are using this guide in a group, you can choose from options 4, 5, 6 or 7. If you have 45-60 minutes for study and discussion in each group meeting, then you can use option 5. Or if you have only 30 minutes available, you can use option 4. These options allow you to have twelve meetings by breaking at the dividing point in each session and using all the questions, including those with an asterisk.

If your group has only six meeting times available, then follow the column headed "Number of Sessions" down to options 6 and 7. Option 6 provides for 60-minute sessions without the asterisked questions while option 6 allows for 90-minute sessions using all the questions.

Note that there are four plans that allow for in-depth study—options 1, 3, 5 and 7. These use each of the questions and will allow for the most thorough examination of Scripture and of ourselves.

With seven different options available to you, Christian Character Bible Studies offer maximum flexibility to suit your schedule and needs.

Each study is composed of three sections: an introduction with a question of approach to the topic of the day, questions that invite study of the passage or passages, and leader's notes at the back of the book. The section of questions provides space for writing observations, either in preparation for the study or during the course of the discussion. This space can form a permanent record of your thoughts and spiritual progress.

Suggestions for Individual Study

1. Read the introduction. Consider the opening question, and make notes about your responses to it.

2. Pray, asking God to speak to you from his Word about this particular topic.

3. Read the passage in a modern translation of the Bible, marking phrases that seem important. Note in the margin any questions that come to your mind as you read.

4. Use the questions from the study guide to more thoroughly examine the passage. (Questions are phrased from the New International Version of the Bible.) Note your findings in the space provided. After you have made your own notes, read the corresponding leader's notes in the back of the book for further insights. (You can ignore the comments about moderating the dynamics of a discussion group.) Consult the bibliography for further information.

5. Re-read the entire passage, making further notes about its general principles and about the personal use you intend to make of them.

6. Pray. Speak to God about insights you have gained into his character—and your own. Tell him of any desires you have for specific growth. Ask his help as you attempt to live out the principles described in that passage.

Suggestions for Group Study

Joining a Bible study group can be a great avenue to spiritual growth. Here are a few guidelines that will help you as you participate in the studies in this guide.

1. These are inductive Bible studies. That means that you will discuss a particular passage of Scripture—in-depth. Only rarely should you refer to other portions of the Bible, and then only at the request of the leader. Of course, the Bible is internally consistent, and other good forms of study draw on that consistency, but inductive Bible study sticks with a single passage and works on it in-depth.

2. These are discussion studies. Questions in this guide aim at helping a group discuss together a passage of Scripture in order to understand its content, meaning and implications. Most people are either natural talkers or natural listeners. Yet this type of study works best if people participate more or less evenly. Try to curb any natural tendency to either excessive talking or excessive quiet. You and the rest of the group will benefit.

3. Most questions in this guide invite a variety of answers. If you disagree with someone else's comment, say so (kindly). Then explain your own point-of-view from the passage before you.

4. Be willing to lead a discussion. Much of the preparation for leading has already been accomplished in the writing of this guide. If you have observed someone else direct the discussion two or three times, you are probably ready to lead.

5. Respect the privacy of others in your group. Many people speak of things within the context of a Bible study/prayer group, that they do not want as public knowledge. Assume that personal information spoken within the group setting is private, unless you are specifically told otherwise. And don't talk about it elsewhere.

6. Enjoy your study. Prepare to grow. God bless.

Suggestions for Group Leaders

Specific suggestions to help you appear in the leader's notes at the back of this guide. Read the opening section of the leader's notes carefully, even if you are only leading one group meeting. Then you can go to the section on the particular study you will lead.

Introducing Loving the World

"For God so loved the world that he gave. . . ."

If God expresses his love for the world by giving, we can expect to do the same. But what shall we give? And how can we show love for a world created by God, but corrupted by sin? How can we love the world, but not become its captors?

This study guide will help you answer those questions. First you will look at the general area of valuing life—a man who valued life so little that he killed his brother, and God who valued life so much that David said to him, "You knit me together in my mother's womb. . . ." And you will ask yourself, if God values life that much, how can I show respect for the lives around me? How can I cope with my own sense of worthlessness?

Next, you will study ways to help the sick and physically disabled—and the risks that come with that kind of service. You will read about King David, who helped a crippled descendant of his rival King Saul and, consequently, paid a price during an attempted coup. And you will follow Jesus as he touched the sick and hurting. Among other questions, you will ask, "How can we help the sick and disabled in ways that preserve independence and dignity?"

God has a heart for the oppressed. Jesus claimed that God sent him to "preach good news to the poor," "proclaim freedom for the prisoners," and "release the oppressed." Then he invites us to shake off our own oppression and exchange it for a bond with him. He says, "Come to me, all you who are weary and burdened . . . take my yoke upon you and learn from me . . . for my yoke is easy and my burden is light." In study three, you will learn to spot the oppressed around you and begin to approach them with God's relief.

Those who love the world, as God does, must learn to practice hospitality. In study four, you will meet Abraham, who spent all day preparing food for three men he'd never met—and listening politely to their absurd prediction about his family life. And you will study a husband-and-wife team, first-century believers, who nurtured a church in their home, provided housing for a religious rabble-rouser named Paul, and then used what Paul had taught them to instruct a confused but highly vocal evangelist. And you will consider how you can use your own home for God's purposes.

Protecting the environment is high on the list of priorities for those who love the world. In study five, you will read a poem that reveals God's own love for what he has made. It includes such lines as "He wraps himself with light as with a garment." You will pray with the prophet Habakkuk who learned that all of the natural beauty of his country was about to be destroyed—by God. And you will marvel at his continued trust in God. You will mourn with the apostle Paul about a creation that groans as "in the pains of childbirth." And you will ask yourself how you can restore some of what God saw as good "in the beginning."

"God so loved the world that he gave *his one and only Son.*" In the final study, you will look at what makes the Christian faith Christian. How is it different from positive feelings about ourselves and the world around us? Why is the Christian faith separate from other world religions? You will have an opportunity to thank God for those who loved you enough to share with you their faith in Jesus. And you will ask how you can show your love for those in the world around you with a generous sharing of your own faith.

May God transform you, as he transforms his world through your love—and his.

Carolyn Nystrom

ONE

VALUING LIFE

Genesis 4:1-24; Psalm 139

Valuing human life wears many colors. Black-and-white photos of thin children in worn clothing dot my husband's suburban classroom. Why? The photos have little to do with math, the subject he teaches to seventh-graders. They are his unspoken contribution to helping affluent thirteen-year-olds become aware of worldwide needs. Thus the pictures. They are of real children gnawed by real hunger. And for some thoughtful teenager, a statistic in a textbook becomes a real life with a human face.

Yet, this same man says of his own life, "If I get cancer, I want no heroics. Just shoot me full of painkillers, and I'll go when my time comes."

My father, on the other hand, says, "Don't let anybody pull the plug on me. I want the full treatment—right to the end. Only God should end my life."

One friend of mine works at an anti-abortion counseling clinic. Another friend campaigns for a woman's rights over the life in her own body. And our family adopted two "unwanted" high-risk children.

My husband votes for candidates who oppose the death penalty. I'm not so sure that the death penalty is always wrong. My mind says that ending a murderer's life may prevent even greater wrongs.

A long-experienced counselor of troubled teens tells me, "I'm tired of hearing the 'I'm going to kill myself' threat. I just tell them, 'Go ahead and do it. I'll read about it in the paper.' " (He's never had to read about it. Something about his blustering, but undeniable, love for them, I suppose.)

For several years, I visited a nursing-home patient in his nineties. Then an illness destroyed his esophagus, so he slowly starved to death—at his own request. Two days before he died, I read to him Psalm 139.

Must we always respect human life? Why? And if we value life, how ought we to show it? Scripture gives us some clues.

Part One

1. In what different ways do people you know show respect for life?

Read Genesis 4:1-24.

2. What symbols of life do you find in verses 1-4?

3. How did the various people in verses 1-4 acknowledge God's presence?

4. Focus on verses 5-8. If you were Cain's defense attorney, what would you say about your client?

5. If you were Cain's prosecutor, what would you say about his crime?

6. Study verses 9-16. In what ways did God, as judge, suit Cain's punishment to both the criminal and the crime?

*7. How was the natural environment of God's creation affected by Cain's sentence (v. 12)?

*8. Look at verses 17-24. In spite of Cain's crime, his life appears to have had lasting value. What did Cain's descendants contribute to culture?

9. How is Lamech's view of life an extension of what you saw in Cain?

*10. In what different ways did God show that he valued life—Abel's and Cain's? (Draw from the entire text.)

*11. Look again at God's conversations with Cain. How might Cain have benefitted, if he had chosen, from his encounter with God?

12. Cain murdered his brother. If you had been their parents, what questions would you be asking yourself?

13. What are some ways that family members can show that they value each other's lives?

Part Two
Read Psalm 139.
*14. What do you appreciate about this poem?

15. What words and phrases here reflect the value God places on human life?

16. Divide the psalm into five stanzas. What is the general subject of each?

17. Take a quick mental survey of what you have said and done in

the past twenty-four hours. How do the words of verses 1-6 make you feel about yourself?

about God?

*18. Why might a person want to run from God?

19. In what different ways do verses 7-12 illustrate God's constant presence?

20. Focus on verses 13-18. What words and phrases here show how much God cares about your life?

21. Do a quick calculation of the number of days you have lived thus far. Verse 16 says that God wrote each one of those days in his book before even one of them came to be. How might that knowledge affect the way you feel about your day when you wake up tomorrow morning?

*22. How might this passage help you to cope with the death of someone you love?

*23. Study verses 19-22. In what ways are these four verses different from the rest of the psalm?

24. In view of the many ways that David has expressed a value of life, why do you think that he would ask God, at this point, to *slay* the wicked (v. 19)?

25. Meditate for a few moments on verses 23-24. What do you consider to be key words in these two verses?

26. If you were to ask God to lead you into the "way everlasting," what would you be saying about life—and death?

27. If you, or a friend, were beginning to think that your life was worthless, how might Psalm 139 encourage you?

*optional question

TWO

MEETING PHYSICAL NEEDS

2 Samuel 9; Mark 5

D avid lived in an era when kings killed their competitors. And he'd spent a decade or more on the receiving end of that threat. Saul, the first king of Israel, wanted David dead.

Saul's career had begun well enough. Samuel had anointed him king, and Saul quickly became a military victor. Then he was disobedient to God, and God, speaking through Samuel, rejected Saul as king. The Scripture says, "Samuel mourned for him. And the LORD was grieved that he had made Saul king over Israel." Meanwhile, Saul's actions became those of a man who was not quite sane.

Samuel, acting on God's instructions, anointed David as the next king of Israel. But no one did David the favor of removing Saul from the throne. David worked for Saul, fought his battles, served in his court, became his son Jonathan's best friend. In return, Saul gave David his daughter Michal as wife, "so that she may be a snare to him."

One day while David was providing harp music in the royal court,

Saul became so enraged that he tried to run David through with a spear. David dodged; Saul rammed his spear into a wall. Later, David and Jonathan swore friendship to each other "between your descendants and my descendants forever." They parted never to see each other again.

David became a fugitive. Yet David refused to kill Saul when he had the chance. Meanwhile, Saul decided that his daughter was not doing the job he'd assigned her with David, so he gave her to another man as his wife.

This pattern appears to have gone on for some years. Both Saul and David fought the enemies of Israel, but Saul constantly took side trips to threaten David's life. Eventually, Saul engaged a battle with the Philistines that was far too big for him. Three of his sons, including Jonathan, died in the fight. Saul, mortally wounded, took his own life. And David was king.

But David ruled a kingdom of divided loyalties and with enemies on every border. It would have been politically smart to kill or deport Saul's remaining relatives, and to strip officials who favored him from power. Instead, David asked, "Is there anyone still left of the house of Saul to whom I can show kindness for Jonathan's sake?" And he found Mephibosheth, a cripple.

Part One
1. If you were unable to walk, what kind of help would you want— and not want?

*2. When you are with someone who is disabled, what do you worry about?

Read 2 Samuel 4:4 and 2 Samuel 9.
*3. Mephibosheth referred to himself in verse 8 as a "dead dog."
What would be difficult about his disability in that era?

4. In what practical ways did David show kindness to Mephibosheth?

*5. What did David do that allowed Mephibosheth to maintain a
sense of dignity? (Find all that you can.)

6. What did David risk by taking Mephibosheth and Ziba into his
household?

Later David's kingdom suffered an internal rebellion—led by his
own son Absalom. King David had to run from Jerusalem to keep
from being killed. Just as he left, he met Ziba.

Read 2 Samuel 16:1-4.
7. How did Ziba return David's favors?

8. How did Ziba explain his presence and Mephibosheth's absence?

How did David respond?

The rebellion ended. Absalom died. David returned, still in power, to the capital city.

Read 2 Samuel 19:24-30.
9. How did Mephibosheth's story differ from what Ziba had said?

*10. What do you think of David's decision about the fields that had belonged to Saul?

11. If you had been David, with hindsight, would you have helped Mephibosheth in the same way in the beginning? Explain.

12. Quickly list several people that you know who are disabled in some way. None of us can meet all the needs of all the people we know. So select one person from your list. Think what it would cost you to help that person. (Consider time, money, personal risk.) What are you willing to do, that is within the cost you are willing to pay, that would be of genuine help to that person?

Part Two
*13. Jesus talked with and touched sick people that other people left

in isolation. What kinds of ill people today do many people try to avoid?

Read Mark 5.
*14. Find as many demonstrations here as you can of Christ's kindness.

15. Focus on verses 1-20. What words and phrases show the severity of the man's problem?

16. What changes showed that Christ had made him well (vv. 13-20)?

*17. In what ways do you see Satan at work throughout the events here?

18. Why do you think that Jesus would not take the man with him?

*19. Study verses 21-43. Why might Jairus have reasonably expected Jesus to take care of his needs first?

20. Leviticus 15:25-28 says that when a woman has a discharge of blood she is unclean, and anyone who touches her is also unclean. Jesus stopped everything and publicly announced that this woman had touched him. Why would that be hard for her?

21. Why was it also a kindness?

22. In spite of the long wait, in what ways did Jesus show consideration for the needs of the girl and her family in verses 36-43?

23. Because Jesus is God who has all power, Jesus could have made people well by simply standing on a distant hill and naming them. Why do you think he chose to heal in the way that he did?

24. How can you bring Christ's love, in a personal way, to someone who is ill?

*optional question

THREE

RELIEVING THE OPPRESSED

Isaiah 61; Luke 4:14-22; Matthew 11:25-30

*T*he evening news on my living-room TV is full of oppression.
I see an elderly babushka-clad woman standing in line to buy
bread. She has been waiting for five hours.

A reporter speaks of a conference in Chicago that has pulled in
professionals from around the world to study serial killers. But the
Laotian family who immigrated to nearby Milwaukee to escape oppression in their homeland feels more oppressed than ever. Their
fourteen-year-old son was one of the victims.

A nearby prison is in lockdown because of riot. The prisoners
complain of crowded conditions in a complex designed for half their
number. And still, dangerous men and women go free for lack of
space.

Even an ad shows small frail bodies from around the world, tat-
tered clothes, feeding cup in hand, flies crawling over a face, and

asks me with pleading voice to "Save the children."

A phone call interrupts to inform me that a family friend oppressed by long-term mental illness has just lost his job. His seventy-sixth. And this time it wasn't his fault.

Just watching the news from my soft sofa with a cool lemonade in hand pants its own breath of guilt-laden oppression.

Part One

1. If you had unlimited resources, what would you do to relieve the world's oppression?

Read Isaiah 61.

2. Notice the introduction to this chapter in verses 1-2. What kinds of people is God concerned about—and what does he plan to do for them?

*3. Imagine yourself as one of the oppressed people mentioned in verses 1-2. Find one statement in the rest of the chapter that you would want to hear.

4. Ancient Jews mourned death by putting ashes on their heads and making a tear in their clothing. Why might the words of verse 3 be especially important to a person caught in grief?

*5. Verse 3 says, "They will be called oaks of righteousness, a planting of the LORD for the display of his splendor." When have you seen grief result in this kind of good?

6. Examine verses 4-9. If a nation were oppressed, what changes would have to take place for the pictures in these verses to become reality?

7. Verse 6 says, "You will be called priests of the LORD, you will be named ministers of our God." Why might a person who has suffered oppression be a good minister or priest?

8. Study verses 8-9. What hope could an oppressed person find in these words?

*9. Verse 10 begins, "I delight greatly in the LORD." What do you find in verses 10-11 that can cause *you* to delight in the Lord? Explain.

10. Look again at the different kinds of relief from oppression that God provides. How can we imitate God in our own relationships with the oppressed?

*11. Which of the blessings in this chapter do you most want from God for yourself?

Part Two
12. If you were to encounter in an airport a person who was poor, blind, an ex-prisoner, or a refugee from an oppressed country, what would be your instinctive response? Why?

Read Luke 4:14-22.
13. Notice Christ's actions in his community and the responses of the people to him. What does this tell you about Jesus?

14. How would Christ's reputation in the community prepare people to accept the new role that Jesus now described?

15. As you think of Christ's life and work, in what ways can you see that he fulfilled the description from Isaiah 61?

16. How has Christianity (based on Christ's life and teachings) continued the work described in verses 18-19?

*17. When have you been on the giving, or the receiving, end of this kind of ministry?

Read Matthew 11:25-30.
*18. If you were hearing these words for the first time, why might you want to "come to" Jesus?

*19. What words and phrases show that Christ's yoke is both freeing and binding?

*20. How does this passage explain the relationship between Jesus, his Father, and people?

*21. How do you reconcile the tension between verse 27 which says, "No one knows the Father except the Son and those to whom the Son chooses to reveal him," and verse 28 which begins, "Come to me all . . ."?

22. Why might you offer Christ as relief to the oppressed?

23. In what ways does belonging to Christ relieve your own oppression?

*optional question

FOUR

PRACTICING
HOSPITALITY

Genesis 18:1-15; Acts 18

*I*n Leo Tolstoy's short story "What Men Live By," Simon was a none-too-competent shoe cobbler who had trouble collecting his bills and drank away anything he did earn. Simon and his wife shared a single badly worn sheepskin coat and ate bread made from meager cupfuls of their depleted supply of flour.

On a bitter day of Russian winter, Simon dressed in the clothes that he shared with his wife, and tramped out in the snow in an attempt to collect some past-due bills for shoe repair. Instead, he collected only pocket change (which he spent on vodka), and another pair of boots to repair. On the way home, befuddled by alcohol, he saw a naked man leaning against a small shrine. Simon began to stumble past, certain that anything this man needed was far beyond his means to help, but "his conscience began to nip him."

So Simon stopped, took off his belt, threw the ragged sheepskin coat over the man's shoulders, tightened it with the belt, and put the unrepaired boots on the man's feet. He put his hat on the man's head—but took it back when he realized that the strange man had long hair, but that his own bald head was cold. Then he handed the man his walking stick and half-carried him home. Once there, his wife greeted the strange man and her liquor-breathed, but empty-handed, husband with predictable dismay.

The man stayed for six years. What follows is a story of host and guest, of teacher and student. And at times it is hard to say which man played which part. In short-story fashion, the stranger's identity remains a secret until the end.

Tolstoy himself lived by the principles of his story. He was born on a family estate in 1828, but soon orphaned. So he was reared and educated by relatives. By his early forties he had published *War and Peace.* Russian scholars of the era gave him "first place among all our contemporary writers." Tolstoy enjoyed the comforts of that position—a luxurious home, a young wife, thirteen children.

By the time Tolstoy was fifty, however, his conscience began to "nip him." His study of the Scriptures led him to believe that God wanted people to take care of each other and that God despised the oppression of rich against poor. So Tolstoy began to dress like a peasant. He spent time at the manual trade of shoemaking. He gave his estate to his heirs and refused profit from his royalties. He sponsored 250 relief kitchens. In the end, he died—at the age of eighty-two, a guest in a railroad station-master's hut.

Many short stories of Tolstoy's later life deal with the theme of hospitality, and God at work through the host and the guest.

Part One
1. What do you do to prepare for houseguests?

When you are a guest, what helps you to feel comfortable?

Read Genesis 18:1-15.

2. How did Abraham show hospitality? (Find all that you can.)

*3. What effort, time and material goods did Abraham use to make his guests comfortable (vv. 6-8)?

4. Who were Abraham's visitors? (See also Hebrews 13:2.)

*5. Why do you think the three visitors did not make their announcement at the beginning of their visit?

*6. Why did Sarah laugh?

*7. Verse 14 asks, "Is anything too hard for God?" How would you answer that question? Explain.

*8. If you had been Sarah, would you have believed what the visitors said? Explain.

9. Look more carefully at Hebrews 13:2. Why do you think God asks us to be hospitable to "strangers"?

10. What are some ways that people today can meet this command—and still maintain reasonable personal safety?

11. Imagine yourself working the night shift in a homeless shelter. If you expected that each guest was a possible angel in camouflage, what would you do on that shift?

Part Two
***12.** What do you enjoy about your home that you could share with a guest?

Read Acts 18.
13. In what different ways did Priscilla and Aquila show hospitality?

14. Look at this passage with the eyes of a potential host or hostess. Why might Paul be a difficult houseguest?

***15.** What local controversies do you think Paul discussed with Priscilla and Aquila around the kitchen table at night?

*16. What evidence do you see that, in spite of the hostile atmosphere, God was using Paul in Corinth (vv. 8-11)?

17. What do you think Priscilla and Aquila's hospitality contributed to Paul's ability to do God's work in Corinth?

18. What do you think Priscilla and Aquila gained from Paul?

19. Focus on verses 18-28. What further examples of hospitality do you see among the early Christians in this text?

*20. Why do you think Priscilla and Aquila traveled with Paul as far as Ephesus—then stayed there?

21. What reasons did Apollos have to be grateful to Priscilla and Aquila?

22. What are some practical ways that you can use your own home to accomplish God's work?

*optional question

FIVE

PROTECTING
THE ENVIRONMENT

Psalm 104; Habakkuk 3; Romans 8:18-27

One night last summer, I stretched flat on my back in the grass of Trail Ridge Camp Cherith in central Wisconsin. "The stars are great at camp," my kids had all said. I was there to find out.

I had walked past the beam of a barnyard pole light, past the light on the wash-house door, and out into a grassy meadow shrouded in twilight but still exhaling the warmth of afternoon sun. Myriad meadow insects sang their evening prayers. Tiny feet scurried through their own maze-world so deep in the grass that they barely fluttered the seeded canopy above. An owl hooted far away. Children's voices laughed and sang, near enough to carry me music, but too distant to bring me the ever-present turmoil of childhood. A light breeze washed my face clean of sweat.

And stars. They emerged slowly at first, a few in the central heavens, but none near the still-lighted horizon. Could I count them? Almost. Then more and more came out. The first ones glared trumpet-like against the inky black, while others danced a gentle harmony. Even the horizon forgot the glow of sun and took on hundreds of thousands of lesser lights. Constellations, those artificial lines connecting stars like so many games of dot to dot, followed the patterns of my school-girl memory—Orion the Hunter, Cassiopeia the Chair, Leo the Lion, Big Dipper, Little Dipper, Draco the Dragon, and the Milky Way so bright I could have walked upon it. A shooting star streaked across the sky, as if to connect the dots for me in some new constellation. Should I wish upon it?

I prayed instead. But what could I say to a God who had made all this and had somehow created in me the ability to enjoy it? For a long time I lay silent. Perhaps silence was the most sensible part of my prayer.

Part One
1. When have you felt that God's creation helped you to know him?

Read Psalm 104.
2. Find a line in this poem that stirs your imagination. What does this line reveal about God and his creation?

3. Study verses 1-4. How does the sky serve God?

4. Study verses 5-9. What elements of earth's creation show God at work?

5. Study verses 10-18. What relationships does this description of God's creation reveal?

6. Study verses 19-23. How does this stanza express an orderliness to what God has made?

*7. When have you enjoyed some aspect of the natural rhythms described here?

8. Study verses 24-26. As you think about the way the world is structured, what signs do you see of God's wisdom?

9. Study verses 27-30. How do these verses show that God not only created, but also personally takes care of, what he has made?

10. Study verses 31-32. Verse 31 asks that "the LORD rejoice in his works." When God looks at his creation today, what do you think causes him to rejoice?

11. Study verses 33-35. What responses to God are triggered by the psalmist's meditation on creation?

12. As you meditate on what God has made, how would you like to respond to God?

Part Two
13. What environmental problems of today do you worry about?

In about 600 B.C., the prophet Habakkuk complained to God that the people to whom he ministered had become wicked. They were violent, unjust and destructive. They refused to listen to him or to obey God.

God answered Habakkuk's complaint. God told Habakkuk that he would send the Babylonians (who were even less godly than his own people) to destroy the nation of Judah. After Habakkuk heard this shocking news, he meditated on his beautiful land and its upcoming destruction. Then he wrote the prayer in Habakkuk 3.

*Read Habakkuk 3:1-15.
*14. Find as many references as you can to the natural environment.

*15. What connections did Habakkuk see between God and nature?

*16. Habakkuk prayed in verse 2, "In wrath remember mercy." What do you think he meant by that request?

*17. Study the last line of verse 6 and the first two lines of verse 13. How might these words help you understand what appears to be senseless destruction?

*18. If you could somehow know that your own nation would soon look like the description in Habakkuk 3, how do you think you would respond to God?

*Read Habakkuk 3:16-19.
*19. How might these words bring stability to you in a time of environmental distress?

In the book of Romans, the apostle Paul wrote an outline of the Christian faith for people who had learned of Christianity by only brief word-of-mouth fragments. In this book, Paul responds to questions new Christians might ask about the faith. Among them, "Why is a beautiful natural environment that God created so messed up now?"

Read Romans 8:18-25.
20. What explanation does this passage offer for our current less-than-perfect environment (vv. 20-21)?

21. What connections can you see here between God's natural creation and God's human creation?

22. Verses 24 and 25 speak of hope. What hope does this passage offer—hope for ourselves and for our environment?

*23. How might Habakkuk's prayer and Paul's explanation of a creation that "groans" help you to cope with disappointment about a natural environment that is less than perfect?

24. Psalm 104 portrays God's creation as a reflection of God's own glory. What are some practical ways that you can maintain or restore some of that glory in the natural environment under your care?

*optional question

SIX

SHARING YOUR FAITH

John 3:1-21; Colossians 1:15-23

My faith is a gift—a gift from God and a gift from the people who gave me a portion of their own.

Dorothy Robbins was co-pastor with her husband of the rural Ohio church that I attended with my family between the ages of six and fourteen. I don't remember a single word of her sermons (or any sermon from that era), but I remember Dorothy as a strong woman who preached the gospel with fervor. Dorothy Robbins shared with me the energy of the Christian faith.

John Reno, permanently on crutches because of polio, taught in the public school down the road from the church. He invited teen-agers *and their parents* to his home for a weekly Bible study and prayer. Mr. Reno brooked no tolerance for pat answers and pre-cooked theories. His searching questions kept parent and student alike probing the text for what the Bible really said. John Reno shared with me a Christian faith that stretches the mind and binds generations together.

Lenore Rostron was a grandmotherly gentlewoman in a new community to which I moved. I arrived just in time to be sent to bed with a problem pregnancy, and she brought me light lunches and armloads of Christian books—both of which I devoured. Lenore shared with me a faith of thoughtful printed words and compassionate care.

Maggie and Paul Fromer—my own Priscilla and Aquila—took a casual Christian newly awakened to the possibility of spiritual growth, and taught me. Maggie inched me through Scripture, analyzing each phrase, couching hundreds of questions with the same theme: "If God says this, what will you do, say, think and be as a result?" (How could I have ever thought that faith was mostly an exercise of the mind?) And Paul? Paul taught me to write. Maggie and Paul shared with me a faith that turns thoughts and feelings into capable action.

Bob Harvey, my pastor for nearly two decades, does what must seem mundane to pastors all over the world. He stands in front of our congregation every week and shows us how to worship God. Then he opens the Scripture and speaks, always something fresh (each week!) that touches my soul and draws me to Christ. But Bob's faith is far more than what I see in front of the church on Sunday morning. All week, Bob works in quiet ways to help our people understand and care for each other. When controversy comes (inevitable in any church), Bob searches out a just and compassionate solution. But it is in crisis that Bob's faith is at its best. He has weathered crises of his own—and he keeps on believing. In crisis, he is a shelter of quiet strength. Bob has shared with me a faith that is faithful.

Joel Scandrett, my son-in-law, and widower of our oldest daughter, has shown me a faith that breathes and grows through suffering. Just 26 months into their marriage, Sheri and their unborn child died in a car wreck. In his grief, Joel spoke of a loving Father who watched his own Son die on a cross. And he felt that God understood his suffering. At Christmas, when their baby would have been born, Joel spoke of a deepened love for the infant Christ child. As Joel studies in seminary to prepare for work as a pastor, I see his constant effort to preserve a faith that grows not only from neat rows of reference books in the library stacks, but also from a heart that knows God. Joel has shared with me a faith that loves Jesus.

These few names join dozens, perhaps hundreds, of others—people who have touched my life, for a moment or for years. They met me at times of pain or joy, times of confusion or confidence, times of frenetic work or peaceful leisure. Some hardly knew that they touched me. Others worked at a relationship that consciously grew us both. But for each one, I am thankful. They shared with me a faith that had been their own. And I am better for it.

Part One
1. Most people have heard about the Christian faith from a variety of sources in a variety of ways. Think about a Christian friend who has influenced you. What did that person say or do that impacted your faith?

Read John 3:1-15.
2. If you had been Nicodemus, what ideas here would have grabbed your attention?

*3. What information shows that Nicodemus was ready to hear what Jesus had to say?

4. How important, according to Jesus, is new birth? (Cite verses and phrases.)

*5. How might Christ's illustrations about flesh and wind and a snake help Nicodemus to understand new birth?

*6. What indications do you see that we will have trouble fully understanding new birth (vv. 8-13)?

7. The term "born again" implies transformation—a change that pervades all of our being: our thoughts, feelings, actions, beliefs, hopes, fears. If you consider yourself born again, what are some ways that you see new birth at work in your life?

Read John 3:16-21.
8. Verse 16 begins, "God so loved the world. . ." What do you see in the remaining section of the text that shows how God expresses that love?

9. In view of these verses would you say that human beings start out with a right or a wrong relationship with God (v. 18)? Explain.

10. What can we understand about human nature from Christ's references to light and darkness?

11. Theologians often speak of John 3:16 as the message of Jesus in a nutshell. How does each phrase of that verse help define an essential element of the Christian faith?

*12. Select one phrase from John 3:16. Explain why that particular phrase is important to you.

Part Two
*13. What attracts you to Jesus?

Read Colossians 1:15-20.
14. What words stand out to you as you read this text?

15. Imagine that you are talking with someone totally unfamiliar with the Christian faith. Use these verses to answer the question "Who is Jesus?"

*16. Verse 15 begins, "He [Jesus] is the image of the invisible God."

What does it mean to be an image of someone who is invisible?

17. Study verses 16-17. How are these verses a good response to the theory that Jesus was a great teacher, a good man—but merely a man?

18. Verse 15 speaks of Jesus as the "firstborn over all creation" while verse 18 says that he is "firstborn from among the dead." What personal hope comes to you because Jesus is "firstborn" in these ways?

*19. Reconcile means, "To cause to be friendly again; to bring back to harmony." In view of verses 19-20, what can you expect to eventually happen to a creation that is now corrupted by sin and pollution?

Read Colossians 1:21-23.
20. Some people say, "I'm not good enough to become a Christian." What reassurance does this passage offer that person?

21. John 3:17 spoke of us as "condemned already." Colossians 1:21 uses the phrase "alienated from God." What does "reconciled" mean to people in that condition?

22. Picture for a moment that future time when Jesus will present you to his Father, "holy in his sight without blemish and free from accusation." What would you want to say to Jesus?

23. Think of a person, not yet a believer, with whom you would like to share that position if you could. What would you like to say to that person now that might lead that person toward faith in Jesus?

*24. Paul ends this section of his letter to the church at Colosse with the summary statement, "This is the gospel. . . ." What, according to this passage, are the essentials of the Christian faith?

*25. At the end of verse 23, Paul says that he is a "servant of the gospel." How could you be a servant of the gospel among the people you know?

*optional question

Leader's Notes

Leading a Bible discussion can be an enjoyable and rewarding experience. But it can also be intimidating—especially if you've never done it before. If this is how you feel, you're in good company. When God asked Moses to lead the Israelites out of Egypt, he replied, "O Lord, please send someone else to do it!" (Ex 4:13). But God's response to all of his servants—including you—is essentially the same: "My grace is sufficient for you" (2 Cor 12:9). There is another reason you should feel encouraged. Leading a Bible discussion is not difficult if you follow certain guidelines. You don't need to be an expert on the Bible or a trained teacher. The suggestions listed below should enable you to effectively and enjoyably fulfill your role as leader. And remember the discussion leader usually learns the most—so lead and grow!

Preparing for the Study

Group leaders can prepare to lead a group by following much the same pattern outlined for individual study at the beginning of this guide. Try to begin preparation far enough in advance for the Spirit of God to begin to use the passage in your own life. Then you will have some idea about what group members will experience as they attempt to live out the passage. Advance preparation will also give your mind time to thoughtfully consider the concepts—probably in odd moments when you least expect it.

Study the flow of the questions. Consider the time available. Plan for an appropriate break (if you are using two sessions) and which optional questions you will use. Note this in your study guide so that you will not feel lost in the middle of the discussion. But be ready to make changes "en route" if the pattern of discussion demands it. Pencil near the questions any information from the leader's section that you don't want to forget. This will eliminate clumsy page turns in the middle of the discussion.

And pray. Pray for each person in the group—by name. Ask that God will prepare that person, just as he is preparing you, to confront the truths of this passage of his Word.

During the Study

1. One of the major jobs of the discussion leader is to pace the study. Don't make your job more difficult by beginning late. So keep an eye on the clock. When the agreed time to begin arrives, launch the study.

2. Take appropriate note of the introductory essay, then ask the approach question. Encourage each of the group members to respond to the question. When everyone is involved in discussing the general topic of the day, you are ready to explore the Scripture.

3. Read the passage aloud, or ask others to read aloud—by paragraphs, not verses. Verse-by-verse reading breaks the flow of thought and reduces understanding. And silent reading often makes concentration difficult, especially for people who are distracted by small noises or who are uncomfortable with group silence. So read aloud—by paragraphs.

4. Keep in mind that the leader's job is to help a group to discover together the content, meaning and implications of a passage of Scripture. People should focus on each other and on the Bible—not necessarily on you. Your job is to moderate a discussion, to keep conversation from lagging, to draw in quiet members, and to pace the study. So encourage multiple responses to questions, and encourage people to interact with each other's observations. Volunteer your own answers only in similar proportion to others in the group.

5. Pacing is a major difficulty for inexperienced leaders. Most group participants have set obligations after a scheduled Bible study. You will earn their thanks if you close the study at a predictable time. But to do so you don't want to race ahead and miss details in the early questions; nor do you want to play catch-up at the end: skipping sections people most want to talk about. Try writing in your study guide the time that you hope to finish questions at various points in the study. This will help you keep a steady pace. Note also any optional questions that you can add or subtract, depending on the pace of the study. But be alert to particular needs and interests in the group. Sometimes you should abandon even the best-laid plans in order to tend to these.

6. If possible, spend time talking about personal needs and praying together. Many groups begin or end by speaking of various worries, concerns, reasons for thanksgiving—or just their plans for the week. Groups who pray together often see God at work in ways far beyond their expectations. It's an excellent way to grow in faith.

7. If you have time, do some further reading on small groups and the dynamics of such groups. For a short, but helpful, overview read *Leading Bible Discussions* by James Nyquist and Jack Kuhatschek (InterVarsity Press). Or for a more in-depth discussion read *Small Group Leaders' Handbook* or *Good Things Come in Small Groups*, both of which are edited by Ron Nicholas (InterVarsity Press). For an excellent study of how small groups can contribute to spiritual growth read *Pilgrims in Progress* by Jim and Carol Plueddemann (Harold Shaw).

The following notes refer to specific studies in the guide:

Study 1. Valuing Life. Genesis 4:1-24; Psalm 139.

Purpose: To value human life—because God does.

Note: Genesis 4 raises a number of questions, not germane to this discussion, but nonetheless troubling to thoughtful students of the Bible. Among them:

□ Why didn't God accept Cain's offering?

□ Where did Cain get his wife?

□ How could Enoch (third generation from Adam) build a city?

To discuss these problems would take most of your study time. And you'd not likely solve the problems. But failing to discuss them may leave some people doubting the validity of the entire passage. A wise tack may be to simply acknowledge that these questions exist, pose several possible answers, then move on to the questions in the guide. Use the information below, as needed.

Cain's offering:

□ Cain, himself, was at fault—not just his offering. Verse 5 says, ". . . but on *Cain and his offering* he [God] did not look with favor." Indeed God's subsequent conversations with Cain reveal serious blots in Cain's character. God warns Cain in verse 7 that "sin is crouching at your door." Clearly, Cain did not make an adequate attempt to resist that sin.

□ Cain's offering was also inadequate. *The NIV Study Bible* comments, "The contrast is not between an offering of plant life and an offering of animal life, but between a careless, thoughtless offering and a choice, generous offering."

□ Other authorities say that since Cain's offering contained no blood it was inadequate because it could not pre-figure Christ's death. Leviticus 17:11, a Hebrew law given at a much later time, suggests this possibility.

Cain's wife:

Adam, Eve, Cain and Abel are the only humans mentioned in Scripture up to this point. So who did Cain marry? Here are possible answers:

□ Adam and Eve had numerous unnamed children. (Genesis 5:4-5 says that Adam lived 950 years and that he had other sons and daughters). Cain simply married one of his sisters.

□ Adam and Eve were God's special creation in an earth already populated by human-like beings. Cain married one of these.

Enoch's city:

□ Any answer that satisfies the question of Cain's wife will also treat the question of Enoch's city.

□ The word "son" used in verse 17 may mean "descendant of," therefore placing Enoch far down the genealogical tree from Adam.

□ The word "city" in verse 17 may speak, in a nomadic era, of any grouping of people who decided to settle in one spot, no matter how small that group might be.

Question 1. Use this question to introduce the broad scope of today's topic. Invite each person to participate in some way. If time permits a follow-up question, ask, "What forms of disrespect for life trouble you?" These two questions will give a picture of the interests and tensions that surround this topic for people in your group.

Question 2. Find five or six answers in the text.

Question 3. Notice the words and actions of Eve, Cain and Abel.

Questions 4-5. Let your group be creative here, but be sure that responses do not disagree with information in the text.

Question 6. Be sure to treat both the act and the person as you answer this question.

Question 7. If you need an additional question at this point, ask, "Why do you think that God gave the land such a major role in Cain's punishment?" Then compare the crime of verses 8 and 10, with God's judgment in verses 12-13.

Question 8. Study the occupations reflected in verses 20-22.

Question 9. Compare Cain's words and actions in verses 8-9 with his descendant Lamech's in verses 23-24. Consider the value (or lack of it) that each exhibited for human life. Consider also the nature of the offenses for which each would take a life.

Question 11. Study each of the conversations between God and Cain (vv. 6-7 and 9-16). What opportunities did God present to Cain? How might Cain have responded differently—and for the better?

Question 12. Use this question to explore emotions and practical counsel. Be sensitive to those who experience intense struggle within their own families. (Modern-day Cains and Abels are not unknown.) Be sure that any "advice" does not come as a recipe predicting certain outcome, but as counsel for those caught in a battle that may be far beyond human ability to remedy. After all, even Eve saw her firstborn as a gift from the Lord—at his birth.

If you are dividing this study over two sessions, end session one at this point.

Question 14. Begin session two at this point. Use this question to allow people to express personal responses to this highly personal psalm.

Question 15. Draw a dozen or more responses from throughout the psalm.

Question 16. The psalm may be divided a number of ways. The following is a common division of stanzas: verses 1-6, 7-12, 13-18, 19-22, 23-24. Help your group to give topic/titles to each stanza.

Question 17. If you need a follow-up question at this point, ask, "Do you see these words as a comfort or a threat? Explain." For further discussion, ask, "In view of the first stanza, what would you change, if you could, about what you did in the past twenty four hours?"

Question 21. Read the first sentence of the question, then pause long enough for people to make a quick paper-and-pencil calculation: 365 x the age at the last birthday + the number of days since then + a few extra days for leap years. A rounded-off estimate is fine for the purpose of the question. When everyone has made a calculation to his or her personal satisfaction (no need to reveal it), proceed with the rest of the question.

Question 24. The words of verses 19-22 are so jarring that people who read Psalm 139 at funerals often omit them altogether. Yet these two verses are a logical outgrowth of David's worship of a personal loving God. David has so identified with God that he sees God's enemies as his own. And he is willing to fight them (physically or spiritually) as vigorously as any general on a battlefield.

Even so, his words are tempered by the final stanza. The accusations that he has just made about God's enemies, he now is able to turn on himself. In stanza five, David looks within himself, and asks God to do the same. Is there some remnant of the God-enemy in him? If so, David asks that God find that "offensive way" and lead him "in the way everlasting."

After the End:

Does your group want an informal after-the-lesson discussion? Does it want another session at a later time? If so, the following questions may continue your study of these passages as they relate today's tensions about the value of life.

"What relevance, if any, do you think these two passages have to such current value-of-life issues as: world hunger, the death penalty, care for the aged or terminally ill, euthanasia, abortion, suicide?

"In what practical ways might you reflect a biblical value of life as you contribute to a solution to these problems?"

Study 2. Meeting Physical Needs. 2 Samuel 9; Mark 5.

Purpose: To give of ourselves to the sick and disabled in personal ways that provide genuine assistance and preserve dignity.

Question 1. Use this question to allow group members to imagine themselves in the disabled person's shoes (or wheels). If a handicapped person is a member of your group, now is an excellent opportunity to learn first-hand about that person's needs and desires. As leader, you should let that person know ahead of time the nature of the discussion so that he or she can be prepared to give thoughtful insights to the group.

Question 2. We often tend to avoid the disabled without asking ourselves why. Now is the time to think about motives for avoidance. Possible answers might include:

☐ "I'm afraid of looking at the wrong thing (legs or face). They might think I'm staring at them."

☐ "I'm afraid they will want too much from me, more than I can give—or more than I want to give."

☐ "I'm afraid they will resent my health."

☐ "I'm afraid I'll ask the wrong questions, like 'How did you get crippled?' "

☐ "I'm afraid I really can't help them in any meaningful way."

☐ "I'm afraid that I can't communicate with them—especially if they can't hear or see well, or if they are not at my eye level."

☐ "I'm afraid I'll accidentally hurt them."

Once the group has examined its motives for hesitating to help, people will be more able to realistically appraise their own abilities and to overcome false fears.

Question 4. Draw from the entire passage. Answers to this question will blend gradually into question 5. When that occurs, just ask the question and proceed with the discussion.

Question 5. If the group is slow to catch the implications of David's help, ask these follow-up questions: "Why do you think that David included Ziba in his help to Mephibosheth? And also Saul's land?" "What did Mephibosheth gain by eating at David's table?"

Answers to these questions should show that David provided a means for Mephibosheth to maintain independence, economic security, and dignity. By seating him at the king's table, David gave Mephibosheth respect, acceptance in the eyes of the people, protection, constant communication, not to mention adequate diet. (Eating at David's table also allowed surveillance, not an unwise decision in view of the events that follow.)

Question 6. In answering this question, consider the obvious personal and economic risks, but also the political risks reflected in the introduction to this study. David had some of the same reasons to fear helping Mephibosheth that we fear in our own contacts with people who are disabled.

Someone will probably notice the last sentence of verse 10. Ziba's household was no small force of able-bodied men. David must have wondered if he could count on their loyalty—and what might happen to him if they turned against him.

Question 10. Let your group discuss reactions to David's decision. Some may think that Mephiboseth, a "johnny come lately," should have lost his share of the inheritance. Others may say that Ziba was lying and should have been banished. Still others may agree with David. He couldn't know which man was telling the truth, so he was right in dividing the property between them.

Question 11. Encourage several responses here, but don't expect agreement.

Question 12. Encourage at least one realistic response from each person in the group. We can't take over a disabled person's life, nor would that person want us to. And we can't solve all of his or her problems. Aim for answers that preserve independence and dignity—as David did. Be aware that any help will entail risk, if nothing more, the risk of rejection. Here are some possible answers:

☐ I will visit a nursing home this week and ask the staff there to suggest someone who rarely has visitors.

☐ I will talk this Sunday with the new person in our church who comes in a wheelchair. I will invite him to dinner at our home with some other friends from church.

☐ I will speak with the wife of a man I know who has Alzheimer's Disease. I'll see if she needs help in planning her future employment and her finances.

If you are dividing this study into two sections, end session one at this point.

Question 13. Begin session two with this question. Many sick people fall into categories that we prefer to leave alone. Among them are AIDS patients, terminally ill, handicapped infants, mental patients, the elderly.

Question 14. Use this question to survey the passage. (Try asking the question just before you read.) Listeners can be watching for Christ's small acts of kindness as well as the obvious large ones of healing.

Question 15. Study the details of verses 1-13.

For some, the description of demons in the Gospels raises red flags about the truth of Scripture. Who were these supernatural beings? Were they real or imagined? Were they an ancient writer's attempt to describe mental illness? Are demons still active today?

This study will not answer questions like these. For the purposes of this study, it is sufficient to notice that Mark, the Gospel writer, believed in demons, that the description of this man (and his healing) is not like what we know of contemporary mental illness, that Christ addressed the demons separately from the man, and that Christ exercised power over the demons. To go much beyond this information in the discussion of demons will probably detract from the general thrust of the study, and from the passage itself.

Question 17. Recall the initial condition of the man—so violent that people weighted him with heavy chains to try to slow him down. Notice also the way the people treated the man, a further influence of Satan. In addition, the conversation between Jesus and the man, with the demons bargaining for bodies, illustrates Satan's work. Notice also that the demons correctly identified Jesus, though the people did not seem to know him as the "Son of the Most High God." Beyond the condition of the man, notice also the work of Satan in the subsequent events—the fear of the people *after* the man was made well, and their asking Jesus to leave, thereby cutting themselves off from his further teaching.

Question 18. Notice the reasons Christ gave in verse 19. Sending the man home was a kindness to him and to his family. If he did not remain, the people there would always wonder if his healing was a temporary "good day." Only as the days rolled into weeks would people see that Christ's work was permanent. In addition, since the people had requested that Jesus leave, the man's presence would be a constant visual evidence of who Jesus is. The man must have done his work well. Mark 7:31-35 shows that at his next visit Jesus found ready listeners in Decapolis.

Question 19. Jairus had reason to feel surprised that Jesus allowed interruption. Jairus was a synagogue ruler, possibly the most important religious leader in the town; the woman was an outcast. Jairus' daughter was dying; the woman had a chronic illness that could be treated at a later time. Jairus had asked publicly for help; the woman wanted anonymity. Jairus was in a position of potential influence for Christ's cause; the woman had been isolated from people for twelve years. In spite of these reasonable objections, Jesus chose to speak first with the woman.

Question 21. Jesus gave public recognition of touch to a woman who had, by law, gone without touch for twelve years. To one who, by law, must live away from other people (so that they would not touch her by accident) Jesus proclaimed, before a crowd, that she was well. Embarrassing, but a kindness beyond all she could have hoped.

Question 22. Notice the practical notes of kindness throughout verses 35-43.

Question 23. Jesus could have healed people without seeing them, or speaking to them, or touching them. Why did he choose to heal them in such a personal way? Let your group discuss the benefits to the people and to Christ's followers. This should lead us to consider ways that we can help people who are suffering. We can write a check and send it through the mail, but we can also. . . .

Question 24. Use this question to discuss ways of overcoming our hesitations and imitating Christ with close personal ministry that comforts both body and soul. See also the note on question 13.

Study 3. Relieving the Oppressed. Isaiah 61; Luke 4:14-22; Matthew 11:25-30.

Purpose: To adopt God's values toward the oppressed in our attitudes and actions.

Question 1. Try to involve each person with some kind of response. Some may say that they would make little or no effort at relief. Perhaps they see the job as impossible, or not their responsibility. Others may want to help, but have no practical plan. Some may prefer to work intensely with only one or two people. Others may try to reshape nations or the criminal justice system. Don't spend all of your time here. Just whet appetites for the job at hand.

Question 2. Note all of the details of verses 1 and 2.

Question 3. Invite a variety of responses.

Question 5. We automatically think of grief as an individual emotion. But answers to this question might also include a community, a nation or a church. One biblical example occurs in John 9 where observers question Jesus about the reason why a man had been born blind. Jesus replied, "Neither this man nor his parents sinned, but this happened so that the work of God might be displayed in his life." The healed blind man then proceeded to make that work of God evident as he disputed with the Pharisees, then confessed his faith to Jesus.

Question 6. Use this question to thoroughly study verses 4-9. Discuss possible changes in the people, in the oppressors, in surrounding nations. These changes should include attitudes and emotions, as well as actions.

Question 7. Your group may pose a variety of qualities that might grow from a person whom God had brought through oppression. This person would experience dependence on God. He or she would understand suffering, and not expect too much good in the world, with the resulting false optimism. This minister would know the strength of evil forces. If you want a follow-up question, ask, "Describe a specific situation where you think personal experience with oppression might be an advantage to a pastor."

Question 10. Guide the discussion so that it deals with attitudes and feelings toward the oppressed then moves to specific and practical actions that would reflect God's values.

Question 11. Invite each person to participate in this question. Make notes of each response. Then, if it seems appropriate for this group, pray together, allowing people to pray for the needs of each other. Refer to your notes so that no need is left unmentioned.

If you are dividing the lesson into two sessions, end session one at this point.

Question 12. Encourage honest answers here. Very few of us have a godly first reaction to these people. And airports catch us at busy, preoccupied times. To discuss our natural inclination at this point, will help to gain a realistic view of the effort needed for any change.

Question 13. Find a half dozen or more actions and responses in the text. Then discuss what these say about Christ's nature.

Question 14. If the group has not noticed, remind people that Christ quoted Isaiah 61, the text of your previous study.

Questions 15-16. Help your group cite as many specific examples as possible.

Question 17. Some may feel that they have had no contact with either giving or receiving this kind of help. If so, ask why. Some may be convicted that they have purposely sheltered themselves too much.

Question 19. Several words in verses 28-30 express binding or obligation: "yoke," "learn," "burden." Others express freedom: the offer is relief for the "weary" and "burdened." Related words are "rest," "gentle," "humble," "easy," "light." An ancient farmer would place his oxen in a yoke. The yoke signaled that the oxen belonged to him. No one else could work the team without his permission. And they were not free to roam on their own. Yet, the yoke enabled them to work for their owner in a safe and efficient way. In that sense it was a protection. It freed them from serious harm.

Question 20. Use this question to study details. Look particularly for connecting phrases between Jesus and his Father and people. Notice also that God is "Lord of heaven and earth." And that includes a lot of people.

Question 21. This question points out the biblical tension between God's power and human choice. Here Christ expresses them both, side by side, in the text. There are no easy answers to this dilemma, but discussing the question will help point out both aspects of a whole that Scripture says is "truth."

Question 22. Who is oppressed? Consider physical, spiritual, mental oppression.

Question 23. If you want an additional application question at this point, ask, "What current burdens make you grateful for Christ's yoke?"

Study 4. Practicing Hospitality. Genesis 18: 1-15; Acts 18.

Purpose: To study biblical examples of hospitality among God's people and to imitate these in our own settings.

Question 1. Discuss favorite symbols of hospitality: clean sheets on the bed, a hug at the door, an un-harried host or hostess, allowing the guest to participate in family routine. Expect different preferences from different people. You may discover that some of your frantic preparations are not significant to many guests.

Question 2. You can gather multiple answers from each of the first eight verses.

Question 3. *The NIV Study Bible* says that three seahs of fine flour was about 20 quarts!

Question 4. Genesis 18:1 identifies one of the visitors as "the LORD." Did Christ appear in human form to Abraham two thousand years before his Bethlehem birth? If so, this is what theologians call a "theophany"—a human appearance of the pre-incarnate Christ. Hebrews 13:2 speaks of "angels." Many scholars believe that the Hebrews passage refers to Abraham's hospitality to these three strangers: Christ and two of his angels.

Question 5. If the visitors had made their announcement first, would Abraham have entertained them differently? for different reasons? Since he did not at first know the identity of his visitors, or their message, what was his motive for such lavish hospitality? Was this his normal way of treating strangers? What does this say of his character? What does his treatment of the strangers say about his ability to be a good father? Discussion of question 5 could lead to these questions and some of their answers.

Question 6. Was Sarah's laugh a laugh of disbelief or of pleasure? Experts disagree. Let your group discuss the options, being sure that opinions do not conflict with the text of verses 10-15. People familiar with the Genesis story will recall that this is not the first time that Sarah had heard that she would have a child (though it was the first time with a timetable attached). Previous announcements appear in Genesis 12:7; 13:14-17; 15:4-6; 15:17-21; 17:1-18. In fairness to Sarah, however, each of these announcements came to Abraham—not to her. And the last time her husband had heard that promise, he laughed too (17:17).

Question 7. For a follow-up question, ask, "Even if you believe that God has all power, what limitations do you place on your expectations of him? Why?"

Question 8. According to Genesis 17:17, Sarah was 90 years old and Abraham was 100. (They lived to be 127 and 175 respectively.) Discuss the obvious reasons for doubt. Then refer to Genesis 21:1-3 for a quick view of the laughter "one year later."

Question 9. Any number of reasons come from biblical principles. Among them:

☐ Hospitality to strangers gives little opportunity for returning the favor. Thus we are less tempted to serve from selfish motives.

☐ Strangers *need* help.

☐ God cares about aliens, strangers, homeless, and instructs his people to do the same (Ex 23:9; Lev 19:9-10).

☐ Christ was a "stranger" in Bethlehem and needed the innkeeper's hospitality (Lk 2:4-7).

☐ God's people are strangers living in a world full of alien values. Our true home is in heaven (1 Pet 2:11).

These and other biblical principles may help your group discuss this question.

Question 10. Your group may have a variety of practical answers. We can provide housing for international students, work in a soup kitchen or a homeless shelter, provide foster or adoptive care for needy children, advocate adequate social services for the homeless, provide an extra home for our children's friends, give supplies and money to people who work directly with the "strangers" of the world.

Question 11. If you are dividing your study into two sections, end session one after this question.

Question 12. Encourage unanimous participation. Even those who live in a single room or dormitory will have something that they can share—a view, a book, a favorite TV show, a neighborhood cafe.

Question 13. Survey the passage. See especially Acts 18:2-3, 26.

For more information and an added dimension for the study, you may also want to read Romans 16:3-5 after you read Acts 18, and consider those verses as you respond to the questions in this portion of the study.

Question 14. Study the details of Paul's stay in Corinth (Acts 18:1-17). Try to see Paul's visit through the eyes of a potential host or hostess. Paul's stay was long (more than a year and a half). He was stubborn, abrasive, a constant source of controversy, with many enemies. Examine the text for examples of what it must have been like to have Paul as a houseguest.

Question 15. Discuss the controversies in the text through verse 17.

Questions 17-18. Discuss the mutual benefit of this long stay together. Use a little sanctified imagination as you discuss their practical and spiritual contributions to each other. Be sure that any speculations do not disagree with the text.

Note on Paul's work in Corinth and Ephesus: Paul taught about Jesus on three missionary journeys spread over about twenty years. Yet his longest visits were centered around two cities. On his second trip, Paul spent nearly two years in Corinth, a Greek cultural and religious center. (Corinth was also known as a sexual playground.) On his third trip, Paul spent nearly three years in Ephesus, a Turkish port city just two hundred miles across the Aegean Sea from Corinth. While these trips become well-defined on a map, the biblical text almost merges them as one. Acts 18:22 ends the second trip, and Acts 18:23 begins the third. Meanwhile, Priscilla and Aquila, who hosted Paul's center of ministry in Corinth on the second trip, form a connecting link as they awaited his arrival in Ephesus.

Question 19. See verses 20, 26 and 27. From these examples we see that first-century hospitality among Christians was common. In fact, Paul probably stayed with other believers throughout his route.

Question 21. Study verses 24-28. For Apollos, Priscilla and Aquila went beyond mere bed-and-breakfast service. They noticed the educational and spiritual gaps in Apollos—and tutored him. (Living and traveling with the apostle Paul gave them more than adequate teaching credentials.) Then they arranged further hospitality for him as Apollos took up his own missionary work.

If you read Romans 16:3-5, you might add the question: "What would be difficult about having a church meet in your home?"

Question 22. Encourage practical and personal responses to this question.

Study 5. Protecting the Environment. Psalm 104; Habakkuk 3; Romans 8:18-27.

Purpose: To appreciate the glory of God's creation, to expect imperfections in our current environment, and to do what we can to maintain what is good in the natural world around us.

Question 1. Your group may need a moment or two of thoughtful reflection before answering this question. Then gather several responses.

Much of the beauty of Psalm 104 is in its vivid images and in the sound of its words. Help the group experience this by taking time to prepare to read (and listen to) the poem. Assign each person a stanza to read, then allow a few moments of silence for each person to read and study the assigned stanza. Then read aloud, listening to each other. Use the following stanza breaks: 1-4, 5-9, 10-18, 19-23, 24-26, 27-30, 31-32, 33-35.

Question 2. Encourage each person to comment in some way.

Question 3. Help your group to admire the imagery contained in these verses about God and the heavens that he created. It will be hard to arrive at precise meanings, though these are worthy of discussion. Perhaps the passage is best apprehended, not analyzed.

Question 4. These verses contrast with the previous stanza. Instead of the sky or heavens, they speak of earth.

Question 5. Help your group discuss the way various portions of what God has made depend on each other. Use details throughout verses 10-18.

Question 7. Encourage personal reactions to the rhythms of the seasons, the day and night, the rhythms of work and rest. Now is the time to mention a favorite walk at twilight, or a proposal of marriage under a full moon, or the moonlit sparkle of a northwoods snow, or getting up early in the morning and going to work with the working world for the first time.

Question 8. Invite answers from the text as well as from observations of the world around us. For example, one of God's attributes is wisdom; we can see that in the world he created and maintains.

Question 9. Help your group to discuss phrases in the text that show God's personal involvement with the world he made.

Question 11. Your group should discuss words in the text such as: "sing," "all my life," "praise," "meditation," "rejoice," "sinners vanish," and "soul."

Question 12. Encourage thoughtful personal responses. If it seems appropriate, close with brief prayers of worship.

Question 13. If you are treating this lesson in two sessions, begin session two at this point.

Questions 14-15. Use these questions to survey the text. References to nature appear in almost every verse. You can ask these two questions as a single unit, or survey the references to nature first, then come back over the list and examine how God has linked each aspect of nature.

Question 16. Help your group to discuss Habakkuk's request. Habakkuk did not ask God to rescind his promised judgment. To do so might deny God's right to judge what is evil—even in his own people. But Habakkuk reminded God of another of his attributes—mercy. So Habakkuk asks that God, even in his wrath, remember to show mercy. We can only imagine in what practical ways God answered that prayer.

Question 19. Linger on this question long enough to understand the unconditional commitment of Habakkuk's prayer. Notice that Habakkuk's source of joy is not in himself, nor is it in his family, or natural environment (places where we often find our own sense of well-being). Habakkuk's source of joy is in God, whom he calls by three different names, "LORD," "God" and "my Savior." Verse 19 suggests that Habakkuk's trust in God allows him to accept inevitable devastation and to continue to worship God with joy—as though he were a deer on a mountain high above the destruction. This is not mere escapism. (Verse 16 reveals that.) It is an enduring trust in God in the midst of environmental disaster. Habakkuk decrees that even then, God, the creator, is still God.

Help your group discuss how Habakkuk's trust might help them in their own times of environmental stress.

Question 21. Connections between natural creation and human creation appear throughout these verses. For example, creation waits, and so do we (v. 19). Creation is subject to frustration, and so are we (v. 20). Creation waits for liberation, and so do we (v. 21). Creation is subject to decay, and so are we (v. 21). Creation will join us in glorious freedom (v. 21). We groan together with creation (vv. 22-23). We and creation wait eagerly for our redemption (v. 23). Help your group point out these connections and to discuss their meaning.

Question 22. Verses 24-25 show that the nature of hope grows from what we have not yet experienced. (Why hope for what we already have?) But because we (and creation) are deprived of perfection now, we grow in the virtue of hope. What is imperfect now (in ourselves and in creation) God will someday make perfect. Revelation 21:1-5 speaks of this new heaven and new earth where all is perfect, a tone reflected in the original creation account of Genesis 1.

Even though we accept certain environmental imperfections now as an inevitable part of earth's corruption, we may not excuse ourselves of responsibility to care for earth's resources. This observation moves the group into the final questions.

Question 23. Use this question to help your group accept realistic expectations of a decaying environment—that God will someday redeem.

Question 24. Use this question to discuss the "flip side" of the previous question. Discuss a variety of practical ways we can protect and renew the natural environment God has created for our enjoyment and for his glory.

Study 6. Sharing Your Faith. John 3:1-21; Colossians 1:15-23.

Purpose: To understand the essential ingredients of the gospel, and to share it with others.

Question 1. Encourage a response from each person. Some should speak of people who helped them to become Christians. Others should speak of people who shared faith in a way that enabled them to become more mature believers. Others may speak of a shared knowledge of Jesus that has not yet led to commitment. Be sure that it is faith in Jesus Christ that your group addresses at this point. Faith in ourselves, or a general positive mental attitude is not the kind of faith that this study develops. If it seems appropriate, pause for a few moments after discussing this question and ask several people to pray, thanking God for those who have led them to Jesus and for those who have helped them mature as Christians.

Question 2. Use this question to spot key ideas in the passage.

Question 3. See verses 1-2, 4 and 9.

Question 4. See verses 3, 5 and 15. Some group members may bristle at the apparent exclusiveness of Christ's statements here. The leader will probably not help the situation by either apologizing or defending Christ's statements. The words are strong enough to stand for themselves.

Question 5. "Flesh gives birth to flesh" (v. 6) says that the character of those born is determined by its source. Physical birth produces a physical body. But spiritual birth (new birth) produces spiritual life.

"The wind blows wherever it pleases" (v. 8) suggests that the miracle of new birth, like the wind, is beyond human control.

"Just as Moses lifted up the snake in the desert" (v. 14) refers to an event in Israel's history. The people had sinned against God, so God allowed them to be bitten by poisonous snakes. Then God told Moses to lift a snake high on a pole. Those who looked at the snake were made well (see Numbers 21:6-9). Jesus knew that his mission was like that of the snake on a pole. Already he was preparing Nicodemus for the manner and purpose of his death.

Your group will probably come to these or similar conclusions through examination and discussion of the text.

Question 7. Encourage several to respond in honest thoughtful ways.

Question 8. Survey verses 16-21 with this question.

Question 11. Your group should look at such words as "God," "so loved," "world," "gave," "one and only," "Son," "whoever," "believes," "not perish," "eternal life." Discuss how each of these helps define the Christian faith.

Question 12. Encourage several personal responses at this point. If you are dividing this study into two sessions, end session one after this question.

Would your group like to know what happened to Nicodemus? Did he ever respond to the faith Jesus offered? See John 7:50-51 and 19:39-40.

Question 13. Begin the second session here. Encourage several people to contribute to this answer.

Question 14. Use this question to gain an overview of the passage.

Question 15. This paragraph is one of the most lofty descriptions of Jesus in the entire New Testament. Walk your group through the text, discussing it phrase by phrase. Help people translate each concept here into language understandable to a person without inside information about the Christian faith. Questions 16, 17 and 19 are further elaborations on this question. If you have already covered them well with this question, you may summarize your findings or simply skip the question when they come up again. But if concepts are still fuzzy by the time you finish question 15, they may become more clear with the later more-detailed questions.

Question 16. If you need a follow-up question, ask, "What does this statement reveal about God the Father, his Son, and the relationship between them?"

Question 19. *The NIV Study Bible* comments on verse 20 as follows: "*reconcile to himself all things.* Does not mean that Christ by his death has saved all people. . . . When Adam and Eve sinned, not only was the harmony between God and man destroyed, but also disorder came into creation (Romans 8:19-22). So when Christ died on the cross, he made peace possible between God and man, and he restored in principle the harmony in the physical world, though the full realization of the latter will come only when Christ returns." See also Revelation 21:1-4.

Question 20. Encourage several answers. Be sensitive to any in your group who may harbor this same hesitation.

Question 23. Even if you could not say what is on your heart (because the person would not receive it), what would you *like* to say? These heartfelt appeals, phrased aloud in the group, may lead to honest and situation-sensitive words at some later time to the persons we would like to bring to eternity with us.

Question 24. Review the passage at this point making brief note of the gospel essentials.

Question 25. Wait for thoughtful answers of personal commitment.

Carolyn Nystrom lives in St. Charles, Illinois, with her husband, Roger, and an assortment of cats and kids and quilts. She has written over 55 Bible study guides and books for adults and children.

For Further Reading

Aharoni, Yohanan, and Michael Avi-Yonah. *The Macmillan Bible Atlas.* New York: Macmillan, 1977.

Bonhoeffer, Dietrich. *The Cost of Commitment.* New York: Macmillan, 1963.

Bunyan, John. *Pilgrim's Progress.* Moody Classics. Chicago, Ill.: Moody Press, 1984.

Buttrick, George Arthur, gen. ed. *The Interpreter's Bible in Twelve Volumes.* New York and Nashville: Abingdon Press, 1954.

Douglas, J. D. *The New Bible Dictionary.* Grand Rapids, Mich.: Eerdmans, 1962.

Ferguson, Sinclair B., and David F. Wright, eds. *New Dictionary of Theology.* Downers Grove: InterVarsity Press, 1988.

Godet, Frederick Louis. *Commentary on Romans.* Grand Rapids, Mich.: Kregel, 1977.

Guthrie, D., J. A. Motyer, A. M. Stibbs, D. J. Wiseman. *The New Bible Commentary, Revised.* Grand Rapids, Mich.: Eerdmans, 1970.

Hodge, Charles. *Romans.* Edinburgh: The Banner of Truth Trust, 1972.

Kuhatschek, Jack. *Taking the Guesswork out of Applying the Bible.* Downers Grove, Ill.: InterVarsity Press, 1990.

Keil, C. F., and F. Delitzsch. *Commentary on the Old Testament in Ten Volumes.* Grand Rapids, Mich.: Eerdmans, 1980.

Lewis, C. S. *The Screwtape Letters.* Rev. ed. New York: Macmillan, 1982.

Morris, Leon. *The Gospel According to St. Luke.* New Testament Commentaries. Grand Rapids, Mich.: Eerdmans, 1974.

Nicholas, Ron, et al. *Good Things Come in Small Groups.* Downers Grove, Ill.: InterVarsity Press, 1985.

Nicholas, Ron, et al. *Small Group Leaders' Handbook.* Downers Grove, Ill.: InterVarsity Press, 1981.

Nyquist, James, and Jack Kuhatschek. *Leading Bible Discussions.* Downers Grove: InterVarsity Press, 1985.

Nystrom, Carolyn, and Matthew Floding. *Relationships: Face to Face.* Wheaton, Ill.: Harold Shaw, 1986.

Peterson, Eugene. *A Long Obedience in the Same Direction.* Downers Grove, Ill.: InterVarsity Press, 1980.

Plueddemann, Jim and Carol. *Pilgrims in Progress.* Wheaton: Harold Shaw, 1990.

Tenney, Merrill C., gen. ed. *The Zondervan Pictoral Encyclopedia of the Bible.* Grand Rapids, Mich.: Zondervan, 1976.

Tyndale New Testament Commentaries. Grand Rapids, Mich.: Eerdmans.

White, John. *Magnificent Obsession.* Downers Grove, Ill.: InterVarsity Press, rev. 1990.

Christian Character Bible Studies from InterVarsity Press
in 6 or 12 studies for individuals or groups

Deciding Wisely by Bill Syrios. Making tough decisions is part of life. Through these Bible studies, you'll find out how to pray for God's will, listen to his voice and become a wise person. These principles of godly decision-making will enable you to serve God in the decisions you make. 1148-6.

Finding Contentment by Carolyn Nystrom. The contentment that characterizes the Christian life is found in intangibles—trust, love, joy, comfort and hope. The studies in this guide will introduce you to these keys to complete fulfillment in Christ. 1145-1.

Living in the World by Carolyn Nystrom. How do we glorify God in secular work? How should we spend our money? What kind of political involvement should we have? This guide is designed to help us clarify godly values so that we will not be affected by the warped values of the world. 1144-3.

Loving God by Carolyn Nystrom. Studies on how God loves—and how his gracious and stubborn love provide the foundation for our love for him. As we learn to love God as he loves us, we'll learn how to be more who he wants us to be. 1141-9.

Loving One Another by Carolyn Nystrom. This guide will help you to solve your differences with other Christians, learn to worship together, encourage one another and open up to each other. Discover the bond of love between believers that is a joyful tie! 1142-7.

Loving the World by Carolyn Nystrom. God has created a glorious world. Our responsibility is to help preserve and protect it. From valuing the sanctity of life to sharing your faith to helping the oppressed to protecting the environment, these Bible studies will help you discover your role in God's creation. 1143-5.

Pursuing Holiness by Carolyn Nystrom. Character traits such as honesty, self-control, sexual purity and integrity may seem out of date. Yet, God's will for us is that we live holy lives. Through Christ, we can find the strength we need to live in a way that glorifies God. These studies will help you to pursue the traits of holiness. 1147-8.

Staying Faithful by Andrea Sterk Louthan and Howard Louthan. This study guide is about wholehearted commitment to Christ. We will be motivated not only to persevere in Christ, but also to grow by taking the risks that will allow us to move forward in our Christian lives. Discover the power of faithfulness! 1146-X.